WINNERS WANT OTHER TO WIN: The Summing Up

By

Jim Green

Dedicated To:

April and Tod

"HAPPINESS comes from within; it is something we owe to ourselves, not something another person can give or take away"

Jim Green

ISBN-13: 978-1500126384

ISBN-10: 1500126381

PROLOGUE

FOR years I kept a plaque on my desk with
WINNERS WANT OTHERS TO WIN....don't
envy, but rather celebrate other's success--
genuinely celebrating other's worthwhile
achievements and ventures is self-
rewarding...[the antithesis of unrewarding
narcissism] --I have always thought if everyone
adopted this attitude...the world would be a
better place....

The primary purpose of this book is to present a
point of view—a summing up if you wish....

About a year and a half ago I started posting on
FACEBOOK—throwing in my two cents worth
about current events, and other factors—some
agreed, some vehemently disagreed—mostly
Republican ideologues—and excuse the candor,
but the Republican party, today, is down right

scary—extremists, an assortment of certifiable nut cases!

And without getting too dramatic--God help America if the Republicans gain control of the Senate this Fall—it will mean America is in serious trouble—we will be on our way out, folks—to use an analogy---we will be on the "Fall" side of "The Fall of the Roman Empire"—with Citizens United our "sign"….

In the Spring of 2014—I would put the odds at touch and go—with the Koch brothers trying to buy the America our extremists on the Supreme Court put up for sale--our future will be tenuous--but it should not even be close—the Democrats should win hands-down—they just need to remember that they are in a dog fight, with a junk yard dog!

So enough of the pessimism, right, but out of these postings, and a surprise ending, this point of view—agree or disagree---should have clarity.

At 80, one has broad editorial license, and would add that I am an eternal student…with an open mind, and like Seymour in "The Little Shop of Horrors" searching for nourishment with "Feed ME"—but regarding this license have included here are a couple of areas that ordinarily would not appear in a Prologue.

First, is the day I almost changed the world....OK, this is the province of the delusional, but hang out with me a bit....The day was December 9, 2000--but this is getting ahead of the story....

To set this up briefly, in 1988, when Anthony Kennedy was named to the U.S. Supreme Court, by then President Reagan, I complained as loudly as I could to the powers that be in the senate confirmation hearings, regarding his covering up a fraud, a criminal offense—had they investigated this crime [outlined in THE HARVARD BOYS CLUB]—he would never have been confirmed.

As we all know, now, it was Justice Kennedy who signed the order to shut down the vote counting in Florida [that Saturday was Kennedy's "duty" day at the Court], thus guaranteeing the High Court's appointment of George W. to the Presidency in the 2000 presidential election--our democratic form of electing presidents be damned!

To illustrate the significance of Kennedy's appointment, the following is a very possible scenario, had Kennedy *NOT* been confirmed by the Senate for covering up Schwarzer's fraud, a criminal offense:

The votes in Florida are counted and as everyone knows--Al Gore is elected President. The debt is paid down to the benefit of all Americans, and America is spared the same disastrous policies used during the Reagan Administration, which almost destroyed our country.

Further, President Gore actually listened to our counter-terrorist office, and Mossad (Israel's CIA) with the same warning, on August 6, 2001, of an imminent airline attack--and 9-11 was foiled--it never happened….

Also, the War on Iraq never happened, nor the War on Afghanistan, nor the War on Terror—nor the trillions in debt piled on the American people by these un-funded wars!

The house of cards known as the Enron Corporation, collapsed from the efficacy of its own pyramid scheme--on schedule. Several of the Cabinet members in the Bush

Administration, including Dick Cheney, are indicted as co-conspirators in this scheme.

In short, America was not set on its current perilous course, with the collapse of our economy in 2008, and our $17 trillion deficit [including $ 7 trillion in mop up costs]--because Kennedy was denied appointment to the U.S. Supreme Court....and the vote counting in Florida went on on December 9, 2000....and we wouldn't have been left with the mind-shattering question—HOW on Earth, in a democracy, could counting our votes be unconstitutional—the jurisdictional basis asserted in Bush V Gore?

THE other tangent I want to go down briefly is to drill down on the question that is the major thrust of my interest these days:

WHY, regarding our unemployment crisis, do we persist it in staying on a "no one wins" path?

On our current path, the jobless lose, and the market loses.

The following letters, as sent, should bring the issue raised, to light [Apologize for some redundancy, in the interest of clarity]:

President Obama/Council of Economic Advisers:

THE HISTORY OF HOW WE GOT WHERE WE ARE

Following WW II, President Truman signed into law the [FULL] EMPLOYMENT ACT of 1946, to provide employment for our returning troops.

Ironically, half-way around the world, Australia codified into their law an almost identical Bill, and for the same reason—

Difference is—Australia actually put their law into effect, and over the next 30 years it was intrinsic to employment policy in Australia that "anybody wanting to work should be able to find a job"—and save for a brief recession in 1961/62 their unemployment was 2%, or less. This period is still referred to as their "Golden Age", in Australia.

Unforeseen by either country, however, in the mid-1970's the world economy underwent a major paradigm shift as a result of the colliding forces of automation, globalization, technology, etc., reaching a critical mass—in brief, an adjustment towards modernity—From a perverse perspective, we became victims of our success....

The instability caused by this transition, however, resulted in a malaise, and ushered in the ill-winds of greed-driven neo-liberalism with its indifference to unemployment, and the likes of Thatcher and Reagan—and the menace of this greed-driven agenda was exploded by Bush II, resulting in obscene disparities in wealth that persists, and is the cause of much friction between right and left, to this day.

It also ushered in high and pervasive unemployment throughout our market-driven economies, the OECD—with 6% unemployment in Australia now the norm, and double-digit unemployment common throughout the Eurozone, to this day.

As a result of the "malaise", however, the U.S. took an aggressive, pro-active role in addressing the, above, economic shift—and in 1978 President Carter signed into law one of the most important laws in the 20th Century--an expansion of President Truman's full employment, i.e., Pro-Market 15 USC § 3101--

which "authorizes" the creation of a "reservoir of public employees" at any time our unemployment in America exceeds "3%"—

But in spite of 3% unemployment being the threshold point above which unemployment starts undermining the Market—and deficit-neutral HR 870/NTN--this Pro-Market solution has never been implemented.

FULL EMPLOYMENT IS A PRO-MARKET CONCEPT, Amazon/Kindle

Jim Green, Democrat opponent to Lamar Smith, Congress, 2000

Council of Economic Advisers:

Regarding our unemployment crisis—Why we insist on staying on a "no one wins" path, is a puzzlement....

The jobless lose, and the market loses....

Further, high unemployment is a breeding ground for climate change-deniers, terrorism, and crime....

And the economy suffers—The market thrives when we have a robust, employed, consuming workforce….

High Unemployment/Sluggish Recovery is not a non-sequitur….

In short, there is NO upside to unemployment!

Further, unemployment is a "social" problem— with oft dire social consequences---we, as the larger society have a responsibility to address— but we run from this responsibility as if it were AIDS….

In taking stock, a large part of the problem is that we keep trying to make anachronistic beliefs/rules apply, such as the most pernicious belief today: "The market can provide anybody wanting a job, with a job"…

This hasn't been true since the mid-1970's, with high and pervasive unemployment throughout the OECD, since--and given "automation", alone, becomes less and less true as we advance into the 21st Century…..

In finding a solution:

Humphrey-Hawkins [15 USC § 3101] was ahead of its time—when it was signed into law in 1978, by President Carter—Now it is Indispensable to the Effective functioning of our 21st Century economy.

In sum, the path 86% of Americans believe we should be on:

We need to codify into our law The Buffer Stock Employment Model—[an expanding and contracting public workforce, that expands during downturns in our market, and contracts as employees return to the private sector]-- triggered anytime our unemployment rate rises above 3%, as "Authorized" in 15 USC § 3101, and funded by deficit-neutral programs such as HR 870, or The Neighbor-To-Neighbor Job Creation Act [hereafter NTN]: A federally mandated Social Insurance, owned by our employed, to provide a fund to hire/train our unemployed—limited to a 4% of salary policy cost.

Fundamental in framing this model:

1] It is based on the premise that we have far more work that needs to be done in America, than persons to fill these jobs.

2] It must have renewable funding ["jump-start" funding--waiting on the market to kick in" is unworkable, in our 21st Century market economy].

3] It must be deficit-neutral.

FULL EMPLOYMENT IS A PRO-MARKET CONCEPT, Amazon

Jim Green, Democrat opponent to Lamar Smith, TX, 2000

President Obama/Council of Economic Advisers:

The field of Economics is awash in graphs and tables—to tell us the health or ill of our economy, but none, nada which warn us of the danger of how unemployment impacts the bottom line.

High Unemployment [6.7%]/Sluggish Recovery is not a non-sequitur. Our manufacturing is disappearing because people do not buy stuff when they are jobless. The prism this problem is currently being looked through has something to

do with our laws –[the oligarchy] regarding "employees" in America—which still have one foot on the plantation—

As a result of this anachronistic mind-set the Republicans blather on in magical thinking—with the promise that if we cut taxes for the 1%, they will create jobs [and not spend this windfall on a bigger yacht—they promise--wink, wink]; and the Democrats stand on one foot and then the other—as we inch along--waiting on the Market to fix our unemployment crisis—and if the Market fails, the unemployed are out of luck!

The larger point being: We need to change the dialogue—we need to change the message. We need to start showing how unemployment cuts into corporate profits.

We currently have the "legal authorization", on the books , to limit our unemployment to 3% [15 USC § 3101]--i.e., at no time should our unemployment exceed 3%--but given the mind-set in Washington, today, it might as well be written in Greek. Congressman Conyer's deficit-neutral, Pro-Market HR 870 never got out of Committee, while it should be voted on today—given our highest priority—and while unlikely, the Republicans might get on board if we shifted the emphasis.

This is a case where the American people are way ahead of Washington…86 % believe that "anybody wanting to work should be able to find a job"—i.e., 15 USC § 3101 has solid political support--Washington just isn't listening.

Given "automation" alone, an expanding and contracting public workforce is an INDISPENSABLE component to the EFFECTIVE functioning of our 21st Century economy—and we need to introduce into our dialogue, IMHO:

> "3% is the zero-sum threshold above which unemployment starts undermining the Market--and the loss in income to the Market is compounded exponentially with each percentage point of increase in unemployment, above 3%".

Jim Green, Democrat candidate for Congress, Dist 21, TX, 2000

Council of Economic Advisers:

The flaw is the belief: "The market can provide anybody wanting a job, with a job".

This is not limited to Washington, and is prevalent in economic thought, today. It has a kinship to standing on one foot and then the other waiting on Santa Claus—rather than accepting, there is no Santa Claus....

What we do know is that in a best case scenario, and given the market doesn't fail—the CBO projects we will return to an anemic 5.5% by 2017—However, the 6/6/14 DOL is optimistic and we may be able to cut a year off of that....

The question that doesn't appear to be on the table, however, is: We have the legal "authorization", on the books [15 USC § 3101], to limit our unemployment to 3%--so why do we have an unemployment rate more than double that--i.e, why is our unemployment rate no greater than 3%?

"High and persistent unemployment has pervaded almost every OECD country since the mid-1970's", Dr. William F. Mitchell, and given automation, alone, this "social/economic" problem becomes even more pronounced going forward.

And yet, aside from Representative Conyers [HR 870]—there does not appear to any program on the table to reduce our unemployment to 3%.

86% of Americans believe: "Anybody wanting to work should be able to find a job"—so it is not the lack of political will standing in the way.

And the market thrives when we have a robust, employed, consuming workforce—High Unemployment/Sluggish Recovery is not a non-sequitur

Currently, No one wins—the jobless lose, and the market loses.

In short, we have an extremely serious socio-economic problem, and we have the means to solve it—so what is standing in the way? And certainly not unmindful of the political climate in Washington—but the real culprit, asserted here, is the anachronistic belief, [and by no means limited to Washington]:

"The market can provide anybody wanting a job, with a job". It is untrue, today, and becomes exponentially less true going forward in the 21st Century—world travel was out of the question when prevailing thought had it that the world was flat.

FULL EMPLOYMENT IS A PRO-MARKET CONCEPT, Amazon/Kindle

Jim Green, Democrat opponent to Lamar Smith, Congress, 2000

Closing out this issue with a law I crafted—in search of the graphs and tables noted above--for our friends in Economics, in academe:

3% is the zero-sum threshold above which unemployment triggers inflation by diminishing labor training and skills, under-utilizing capital resources, reducing the rate of productivity advance, increasing unit labor costs, and reducing the general supply of goods and services-- and the loss in income to the Market is compounded exponentially with each

percentage point of increase in unemployment, above 3%.

People who write have stuff they want to get out—the missives, and miscellany, here, is stuff I wanted to get out….

A few closing comments in the Prologue—the FACEBOOK POSTINGS is to fill in the blank spots--The entirety in this effort is divided into just four chapters—As Oscar Wilde averred "The only truly worthless opinion is an unbiased one"—so bias, agreed—but always in the interest in getting at the larger goal—the truth….

Incidentally, I published my first book on my 78th birthday—and not that I write that fast, or well—the materials were all there for the better part of the past 30 years, give or take, gathering dust—it was just a matter of pulling them together in some order—also, don't believe any book should be over 60 pages, plus/minus—[this book is an exception, of course] i.e., can be read in the crapper--two hours, max--lol—but it seems best summed up by a very astute observer [wish I could recall their name to give credit]: Persons who write do so because they have no choice [it is a compulsion, an addiction..]—they become an "author", however, when people start reading what they have written....

Finally, a note to the reader—the papers and letters are not in sequence, and apologize for redundancy [please look for the nuggets...Thx--lol]—also, if you are a "typo-wonk"—are more concerned with sentence structure, etc., than content—you probably won't like my writing—and you will find a wayward capital letter, here and there, and appearing out of place and used for emphasis—I chalk up to editorial license and tongue-in-cheek, self-effacing humor—so apologies, here—[I seriously support: Take what you do seriously, but never yourself....]....

Just look for content, please....THX

CHAPTER ONE

FACEBOOK POSTINGS:

[The following are pasted—as posted—apologize for the reference to books on Amazon—but oft the book title is tied in to the subject—Also not in sequence, and if appear fragmented they are often a response to another post--but topical to the time—for news-wonks, like the writer, the time-frame will be obvious—a brief disclaimer....some of this stuff is pretty inflammatory, raw--a bit pugilistic—but a sad necessity in today's political climate----does not speak kindly of our current Republican radical extremists—with their devious un-American agenda—also warts and all....look for the nuggets--lol] and shows my outrage against the lack of what Bill Clinton observed about "Conventional Wisdom"/ Washington----"Common sense isn't very common"--THX]

Every Democrat I know is a Capitalist....build a better widget, sell it or a million bucks, and retire in South Florida....but that doesn't include destroying the Earth by drilling the

Rockies down to an anthill—FOR PURE GREED—or supporting that for a JOB....this is lunacy! And this is what distinguishes Democrats from Republicans, today! IT IS IMPOSSIBLE TO BE A CHRISTIAN, AND VOTE REPUBLICAN, Amazon/Kindle

~

RE Income Inequality—the late Peter Drucker urged CEO's salaries of no greater than 20 times that of their lowest paid employee. Switzerland recently advocated a limit of 12 times—in the U.S., today, 300-400 times is common...the naysayers wave and flail that we would have a "brain drain" with a 20 times limit. Really? Where would they go if it was a law? See: OUR GREED AND IGNORANCE, Amazon

~

The world, today, has been turned on its head with the internet—and we now have the opportunity to have wonderful intellectual exchanges with persons from all over the world....and then we run into the person who has "chopped liver for brain" who babbles on incoherently with absolute nonsense and when they learn you are a Democrat—not infrequently, they will call you a "baby killer" which makes you realize why the Republican Party has been taken over by Racists and Radical NUT CASES! See: OUR GREED AND IGNORANCE, and IT IS IMPOSSIBLE TO BE A CHRISTIAN, AND VOTE REPUBLICAN, on Amazon

~

Two groups who totally mystify me—by voting Republican—are Veterans, and Christians—for Vets, who do they think codified the GI Bill, etc., and it is only the Democrats who have stood behind our Vets—the Republicans voted to cut $4.5 billion from Vets benefits—AND, the Republicans stand for everything Christ spoke out against—Christ didn't say steal from the poor to give to the rich! If one is NOT following the teachings of Christ—they are not a Christian! Period! See: IT IS IMPOSSIBLE TO BE A CHRISTIAN, AND VOTE REPUBLICAN, Amazon

~

Were it not for Social Security Insurance and Military Retirement moneys percolating up through our economy—CAPITALISM IN AMERICA WOULD FOLD LIKE A CHEAP TENT! So WHY, on Earth would anyone in their right mind vote Republican—BECAUSE THEY WANT TO DO AWAY WITH BOTH! See: IT IS IMPOSSIBLE TO BE A CHRISTIAN, AND VOTE REPUBLICAN, on Amazon/Kindle

~

America is currently the victim of our xenophobic, homophobic, just plain phobic, and a dash of lunatics—but all of whom enthusiastically embrace the label "conservative"—and with each election cycle our Republican candidates get more hysterical to be more "conservative" than their opponent—to relegate America back to the 8th Century, BC! Wise up—VOTE DEMOCRAT! See: OUR GREED AND IGNORANCE, Amazon

~

ATTENTION LEGISLATORS/LAWYERS: SINCE the Koch Bros, et al got filthy rich from US—US, the American people—[but for the American people, they wouldn't have their fortune—and thus have a fiduciary obligation to America, and Americans]--They must henceforth contribute equally to EVERY candidate—As an act of patriotism to America—or face a $500,000 fine per violation and/or five years in prison—Where is the law suit? See: IT IS IMPOSSIBLE TO BE A CHRISTIAN, AND VOTE REPUBLICAN, on Amazon/Kindle

~

The Republican agenda is transparent—they use code to disguise GREED, and a TOTAL ABSENCE of DECENCY—claiming these to be Christian/family values, etc. and pandering to our gullible, ignorant, persons with low self-esteem, and to a willing racist faction—In short, the Republicans want an America UNFIT FOR HUMAN HABITATION! See: OUR GREED AND IGNORANCE, on Amazon/Kindle

~

60 MINUTES: THERE IS NO BENGHAZI STORY—QUIT WASTING OUR TIME—The Republicans want our ignorant in America to believe Obama and Clinton sneaked into Libya and killed those folks-—EVERYONE

RATIONAL KNOWS THEY ARE NUTS— END OF STORY!

- **A week later 60 MINUTES apologized for using a discredited source, after getting flack from all sides –[and for listening to Faux]….**

~

I have a $100 Tom Tom "Global Positioning System" [GPS] which alerts me to turn left in half a mile—and why this, or similar, technology was not available—in our search for Flight 370, escapes me! We are spending millions and still may never find this plane—anyone got an explanation for this? See: OUR GREED AND IGNORANCE, on Amazon/Kindle

~

Humans are the most important factor in our economy-—and yet we are treated the most shabbily—we don't send our dog or cat out to buy milk or eggs….but for us humans, our economy wouldn't exist—and yet in America we have 11 million idol….A POOL OF SLAVES:

To Be Used and Discarded "at will" [Amazon]—
furniture in the scheme of things….

~

Let's face it [regardless of how this sorts out]—
Republi-Faux would condemn President Obama
if he cured them of cancer—so their waiving and
flailing "The sky is falling" over the rescue of
Bergdahl is just more of "The little boy who
cried wolf" in their desperation to undermine
the prez—to please our racists! See: OUR
GREED AND IGNORANCE: Poses Far More
of a Threat to America, Than Terrorism, on
Amazon/Kindle

~

FAUX is doing everything it can to rile up our
"unstable"—and their eyes glaze over with the
"I" word, and paid informants—i.e., they have
ginned up a lynch mop mentality with most
buying the FAUX propaganda that the six died
trying to rescue Bergdahl—WHY would they be
trying to "rescue" someone they thought
deserted—unless he didn't desert? The larger
point is: The Army should provide extra
security in moving Bergdahl to San Antonio.
OUR GREED AND IGNROANCE, Amazon

~

RE: CPI--President Obama: A business reporting to the IRS a massive loss on a product--when they made a profit—will be charged with fraud—THEREFORE, it is urged that by Executive Order ANY representation [graph] of Social Security Insurance/Medicare Expense—MUST include a DEDUCTION of the dollars paid in—[Social Security Insurance has historically brought in more than it paid out—is less than zero as a percent of government expense—and is hardly the derisive invention of Republicans—an "entitlement"] Jim Green, Democrat candidate for Congress, 2000 See: OUR GREED AND IGNORANCE, on Amazon/Kindle

~

Jay Leno, Flying around the internet—and being added to at 200 a day clip—is a Petition to RECALL TED CRUZ, IMMEDIATELY – would be curious regarding his response? Scroll down on this petition to see that mainstream has his number—Cruz is a McCarthy lookalike.....a demagogue! Jim Green, candidate for Congress, 2000

- The day Cruz appeared on the Tonight Show—

~

86% of Americans believe that "Anybody willing to work should be able to find a job". We have a Federal Law on the books to make this a reality--15 USC § 3101—it is a Pro-Market concept—So what is our problem—we are a democracy, aren't we? See also: ECONOMIC INCLUSIVISM on Amazon/Kindle

~

SEQUESTER--THE REPUBLICAN DIRTY TRICK: In 1980 our deficit was $60 billion—Using deception, Republicans cut taxes for the 1%, put the revenue shortfall on our deficit, and by 2013 had driven America into a $16 trillion ditch—including mop-up costs for their damage to our economy! NOW THEY WANT TO BLAME AND CUT SOCIAL SECURITY? See: OUR GREED AND IGNORANCE, on Amazon/Kindle

~

The Republican party, and their mouthpiece FAUX, has moved so far to the extreme right that virtually all of their politicians and sneaky creeps who use their position to incite our racists, and literal thinkers [AKA the Tea Party]—i.e. they are devoid of ethics and common decency! To be a Christian, one must follow his teachings—Thus: IT IS IMPOSSIBLE TO A CHRISTIAN, AND VOTE REPUBLICAN

~

A "slave", by definition—is a person without rights—so guess what the Koch Bros/the Republican agenda, today, want as an "employee" in America, today—you got it: A POOL OF SLAVES, To Be Used And Discarded "at will" [Amazon/Kindle]—in short, they still have one foot on the plantation—and why ANYONE would vote Republican, today, defies all rational human thought! OUR GREED AND IGNORANCE, Amazon/Kindle

~

All this waving and flailing of arms by the Republicans/Tea Party—and demagogue McCarthy/Cruz—is not because they think the ACA will not work....BUT RATHER, because they are petrified that it will !
http://pac.petitions.moveon.org/sign/recall-ted-cruz-immediately

~

CNN et al: GET HONEST WITH YOUR POLLS: America has been short-circuited to our lowest common denominator---OUR RACISTS....it caused the Shut Down....it is killing our country....eliminate the racists from our polls on Obamacare, and it has overwhelming acceptance by the American people—
http://www.amazon.com/James-L.-Jim-Green/e/B001KHZIMM/ref=ntt_dp_epwbk_0

~

The Republicans in the House are wallowing ignominy—and are a transparent child having a temper tantrum—they were offered 17 requests for conference on Bills coming over from the Senate over the past 6 months...and rejected every one—and NOW they disingenuously claim to champion this legislation—WHAT JERKS! http://www.amazon.com/James-L.-Jim-Green/e/B001KHZIMM/ref=ntt_dp_epwbk_0

~

ANYONE—Is the new anti-gay law in Arizona, another product of the fascist ALEC organization--like "stand your ground"? The extremists at ALEC will do anything, via their "wedge issues", to distract, and cover up the true Republican agenda, today: Specifically, to lie, cheat and rob to get elected—so they can lie, cheat and rob the American people blind, once elected! See: OUR GREED AND IGNORANCE, on Amazon/Kindle

~

Anyone who thinks the VA flap is new, hasn't watched "Born on the 4th of July" [1970's]—And the Republicans should not say even ONE word—They voted to cut $4.5 billion from veteran benefits--To be a Christian, one must follow his teachings, thus: IT IS IMPOSSIBLE TO BE A CHRISTIAN, AND VOTE REPUBLICAN, Amazon/Kindle

~

Apparently, the medical field is a magnet for persons wanting to get rich, rather than cure the ill…a guest on MSNBC Last Word referred to medical plans from "$1000 a month to $2000" a month—AS IF THIS WERE REASONABLE! This is more than millions of Americans make! Making a "profit" from another's health, should be a criminal offense! See: OUR GREED AND IGNORANCE, on Amazon/Kindle

~

Bergdahl….is a "Sergeant"—Why on earth would the Army promote him if all of the lies the Republican propagandists are spreading, are true? And he "volunteered" to defend America-- if he went AWOL by walking into enemy territory—we need to question his mental health, NOT HIS LOYALTY—OUR GREED AND IGNORANCE, Amazon

~

Based on McConnell, and the current Republicans in Congress: Voting Republican in America, today, means that you want an America unfit or human habitation—an

America degraded by GREED AND
AVARICE...that sanctions stealing from a blind
man's cup—an America that is antithetical to
Christ's teachings, and devoid of all sense of
common decency! See: OUR GREED AND
IGNORANCE, on Amazon/Kindle

~

BILL MAHER: [his guest] Question for
Carter—in 1978 Prez Carter signed into law 15
USC § 3101—and then IGNORED—WHY?
Had he enforced the "legal authorization" in
this law, he would have beat Reagan hands
down—This law, is Pro-Market and needed
even more today than then, it provides that at no
time will our unemployment in America exceed
"3%"—and we can do this without adding a
dime to our deficit, with deficit-neutral--
HR870—See: FULL EMPLOYMENT IS A
PRO-MARKET CONCEPT, Amazon

~

Ted Cruz is what we get when the Koch
brothers buy our candidates—i.e., a jerk, a
clown--who has almost single-handled turned
the Republican /Tea Party into the "Miserable
excuse for a human being party"—There is a

solution to their extremism and lunacy—VOTE DEMOCRAT! To be a Christian, one must follow his teachings, thus: IT IS IMPOSSIBLE TO BE A CHRISTIAN, AND VOTE REPUBLICAN, Amazon

~

BILL MAHER: Rep Michael Burgess, One of the 222 mental midgets in the House, reported that a sonogram found a boy masturbating himself in the womb---if there is not a joke in there—JOKES ARE PASSE—but we now have a number: WE HAVE 222 CERTIFIABLE NUT CASES IN THE HOUSE [voted to abolish Roe v Wade this past week]. See: OUR GREED AND IGNORANCE, on Amazon/Kindle

~

We should never condemn the CEO who closes a plant, when they is losing money—but we should be outraged by a Republican House that is incapable or unwilling to address the "social" problems caused by the loss of jobs! FULL EMPLOYMENT IS A PRO-MARKET CONCEPT, Amazon

~

MEDIA: Boehner [Republicans] believe…..Really Believe…."The market can provide anybody wanting a job, with a job"…that is why he pontificates that we don't need to regulate polluted rivers—but Boehner's "Belief" is a MYTH, a fraud--hasn't been true since the mid-1970's— Expose this FRAUD, and the entire Republican agenda collapses into a pile of dung! See: OUR GREED AND IGNORANCE, on Amazon/Kindle

~

When everyone believed the world was flat—world travel was out of the question…and the same is true of the Republican "Belief" that "The market can provide anybody wanting a job, with a job"—it is BS…hasn't been true since the mid-1970's—but since the Republican agenda is premised on this FRAUD, their solutions are Garbage In, Garbage Out…See: FULL EMPLOYMENT IS A PRO-MARKET CONCEPT, on Amazon/Kindle

~

SO WHERE IS THE MEDIA QUERY: "Just how do you plan on doing that, Mr. Boehner,

Jindal, et al"? Boehner/Republicans claim to be "job creators"—their method, however, involves a lot of PRAYER, i.e., Pander to 1% GREED by cutting their taxes--Allow them to drill the Rockies down to an anthill—and then PRAY this will create jobs—But if the market fails—they say—"Oh well, then the jobless are out of luck"! See: THE HARVARD BOYS CLUB, Amazon

~

I detest the term "American Exceptionalism" because whenever I encountered anyone who tells me they were "exceptional"—I'm thinking, I'm talking to a loser! Persons who are exceptional NEVER proclaim "I'm exceptional"—Imagine Einstein proclaiming this….Further, disingenuous Gingrich [who uses it incessantly] saying to other countries "We are better than you"? OUR GREED AND IGNORANCE, on Amazon/Kindle

~

Boehner/Republicans boast daily that they are "job creators"—So where is the Pulitzer journalist asking "How do you plan on doing that?'—HINT: It is the same unworkable method since 1980—cut taxes for the 1%, and they will create jobs with the extra cash—IT IS BS—the 1% put the extra cash in their pocket—AND CREATED THE GREATEST WEALTH DISPARITY IN AMERICAN HISTORY! See: OUR GREED AND IGNORANCE, Amazon

~

The Republican primaries illuminate why DC is in gridlock--There are no moderate Republicans anymore—only Dumb and Dummer---clones of Clive Bundy, resulting in a House filled with Republican lunatics who want to use the American economy/people as a battering ram, so they can undermine President Obama to the cheers of our racists….See: OUR GREED AND IGNORANCE, Amazon

~

Burning the planet down for a "job"—is patently insane—OUR GREED AND IGNORANCE, Amazon/Kindle

~

RECALL TED CRUZ, IMMEDIATELY! To be delivered to the United States Senate: Ted Cruz does not represent the best interests of Americans, or America--and is not worthy of being in the Senate. Cruz is a McCarthy look-alike, a grandstander and demagogue buffoon— even more dangerous than McCarthy—to America, and Americans— http://pac.petitions.moveon.org/sign/recall-ted-cruz-immediately

~

Chris Hayes—[MSNBC All In--regarding full employment] Agree with your observation 100%--so when are we going to refuse an unemployment rate of 6.7%? We have a law, NOW, which reduces jobless Americans to 3%, AND 86% of Americans agreeing that "anybody willing to work should be able to find a job" [Audacity of Hope]—So when are we going to stop accepting the status quo? A solution is provided in ECONOMIC INCLUSIVISM & FULL EMPLOYMENT IS A PRO-MARKET CONCEPT, on Amazon/Kindle

~

Chuch Todd..Daily Rundown…regarding your polls on healthcare….UNTIL you eliminate those who listen to FOX [PROPAGANDA--Not

the news]—Those with an aversion to facts, and those who don't know what we have now—YOU WILL NOT GET AN ACCURATE PICTURE OF AMERICA'S FAVORABILITY OF THE AFFORDABLE HEALTH CARE ACT—
Bio info: http://www.amazon.com/James-L.-Jim-Green/e/B001KHZIMM/ref=ntt_dp_epwbk_0

~

Right-wing media buzzes with dizzying lunacy! First they pleaded for Sergeant Bergdahl's release—now he is a deserter, and the 5 Taliban are all John Dillingers—the world's worst terrorists [Taliban are NOT terrorists—rather, are attacking us, because we are attacking them]--who will sneak over and get us in the middle of the night....[how will they get here, swim?]—and the Right-Wing get out their video of them swinging on jungle bars—preparing for their attack....Folks, We have enough atom weapons to decimate the world....NO RATIONAL PERSON WOULD VOTE REPUBLICAN!

~

Chuck Todd: Rubio is anti-Global Warming [and the dangers in ignoring] because he **REALLY BELIEVES IT IS ONLY THE MARKET THAT CAN CREATE JOBS.** He has a blind-spot in thinking otherwise and therefore he [as well as many Republicans] talks like a lunatic regarding Climate Change....See: **OUR GREED AND IGNORANCE,** on Amazon/Kindle

~

CNN: For an omitted sub-plot in "Our Nixon", you might find of interest **THE HARVARD BOYS CLUB,** on Amazon/Kindle—it regards a relevant figure in the Watergate Scandal—who was appointed to a federal judgeship, and a little known fact--was also a Hitler Youth—this is not an anti-Harvard book, but rather about 3 of its bad apples, one of the 3 being Anthony Kennedy.

~

The ONLY reason we have high unemployment in America is because of the archaic belief—and insistence by the oligarchy that we have **A POOL OF SLAVES*** to be used and discarded "at will", for our workforce in America—in short, our oligarchy still has one foot on the plantation—to the detriment of our 21st Century economy! FULL EMPLOYMENT IS A PRO-MARKET CONCEPT *Amazon-Kindle

~

CNN CROSSFIRE: in a word, Gingrich is NUTS! I do agree, however, that global warming does not pose America with the greatest threat—rather it is Gingrich, himself, the Republicans in the House—and the Republican agenda of GREED, for the sake of GREED—that poses the greatest threat to America—and, indeed, poses a far greater threat to America than terrorism! See: OUR GREED AND IGNORANCE, on Amazon/Kindle

~

MAHER 7/12/13: The disconnect in our "democracy": "Most Americans believe that anybody willing to work should be able to find a job.."—While inexplicably 25 million are unemployed/underemployed—WHY? ANSWER: We have been inimically brainwashed, duped, into believing the Market will create all the jobs we need—when this has

NEVER been true!: See: FULL
EMPLOYMENT IS A PRO-MARKET
CONCEPT, on Amazon/kindle

~

The only "Pro-Life" persons in America are
those who are opposed to the death penalty, and
war—while the Anti-Choice folks, favor both—
further, they are opposed to women's rights—
and their sole objective is the control of women,
and the anti-Christian agenda of the Republican
party—i.e, they want to relegate America back
to the 8th Century, BC! IT IS IMPOSSIBLE TO
BE A CHRISTIAN, AND VOTE
REPUBLICAN, Amazon

~

CROSSIFRE: Does the trash currently being
cranked out by the Republican Propaganda
Mill: TO DEHUMANIZE President Obama—
and spewed out endlessly by
Gingrich/Limbaugh/SE Cupp, etc.--Such as he is
weak, or lacks leadership, or is like Hitler—
resonate beyond our racists? Or is this profound
stupidity more widespread? A quote by George
Orwell: "During times of universal deceit,
telling the truth becomes a revolutionary act".

See: IT IS IMPOSSIBLE TO BE A CHRISTIAN, AND VOTE REPUBLICAN, Amazon/Kindle

~

Does anyone know the demographics on the percent of our electorate that are Republican/Conservative nut cases? Some are just plain racists—but it is reported to be upward of 40%, and if so, America is in serious trouble—for example, the Republican lunatics in the House that are using the American people as a battering ram to undermine President Obama! See: OUR GREED AND IGNORANCE, on Amazon/Kindle

~

The problem with Will Cain, et al [Republican ideologues]—he doesn't have the foggiest idea how our economy works...i.e., he is ANTI-CAPITALISM! For instance, I am a capitalist—capitalism only works by having a viable interaction with government—Cain et al, wants to make government an adversary—TO THE DETRIMENT OF CAPITALISM. See: FULL EMPLOYMENT IS A PRO-MARKET CONCEPT, on Amazon/Kindle

~

President Obama had a weapon not available to FDR, in their respective economic meltdowns—specifically, were it not for Social Security Insurance moneys percolating up through our economy in 2008-9—we would be not be talking about having narrowly averted another Great Depression in 2008-9—We would be buried in one! See: FULL EMPLOYMENT IS A PRO-MARKET CONCEPT, Amazon

~

Re: the Ogallala Aquifer—we have the technology—and it seems improbable just from the loss of production [$] alone that it would not be used, i.e., an alarm that would immediately target a leak—and why not require an impervious undercover be required for that small corner crossing the aquifer? If our only choices are trucks/trains or pipeline...it is pipeline hands down. See: OUR GREED AND IGNORANCE, on Amazon/Kindle

~

Our Ted twins....Nugent and Cruz...are persons of low character, and even lower quality as human beings—and prove it every time they open their mouth—sign the attached petition and send a message!
http://pac.petitions.moveon.org/sign/recall-ted-cruz-immediately

~

We have the Tea Party, and Egypt has the Muslim Brotherhood—which must offer some comfort to Egypt that they are not alone in extremist nut cases—For Instance, the Tea Party/Cruz want to relegate life in America back to "The Grapes of Wrath"—i.e., to create an America unfit for human habitation! THROW THE BUMS OUT!
http://pac.petitions.moveon.org/sign/recall-ted-cruz-immediately

~

The Democrats are the ONLY real Capitalists in America--DIFFERENCE IS...Democrats know that but for the American people they would not have their wealth—which creates a fiduciary obligation to America—FOR Republicans it is

LIE, CHEAT, AND ROB to get elected, so they can **LIE, CHEAT, AND ROB** the American people blind, once elected! See: **IT IS IMPOSSIBLE TO BE A CHRISTIAN, AND VOTE REPUBLICAN**, Amazon/Kindle

~

Ryan/Cruz, et al--The Tea Party Republicans in Washington—are not human beings…they are insufferable creeps! They set as a **PRIORITY, AGAIN PRIORITY** to cut $40 billion from Food Stamps [to gut the program]—so they could give a $5 billion tax break to Exxon, that is making record profits! And in the process cheated our farmers who are producing the food for our poor! This book title has never been more suited, than here—**IT IS IMPOSSIBLE TO BE A CHRISTIAN, AND VOTE REPUBLICAN**, Amazon/Kindle

~

FELLOW TEXANS/RED STATES: If you are tired of your state being looked upon as a back-water Third World Country—**VOTE DEMOCRAT**—And get rid of the lunatics like Ted Cruz, et al--who have taken over the Republican Party—In short, the GOP is now

being dubbed GREEDY OLD PRICS—
misspelling acknowledged—See: IT IS
IMPOSSIBLE TO BE A CHRISTIAN, AND
VOTE REPUBLICAN, on Amazon/Kindle

~

Find a "Crazy Republican [47%]", and you will
find someone who believes that "sex is a sin"—it
is this belief that is the [excuse] seminal seed in a
building block to an array of faulty logic:
rejecting evolution, anti-Choice, voting
Republican, etc—So where are our studies, and
media expose'? See: IT IS IMPOSSIBLE TO
BE A CHRISTIAN, AND VOTE
REPUBLICAN on Amazon/Kindle

~

Please forward to: Mr. Fred Schepisi: I would
like to call your attention to "The Harvard Boys
Club", on Amazon—a common thread runs
through "A Cry In The Dark", and
"Indictment" re the McMartin pre-school
case—in that all regard innocent, decent people
who are snared into a system that has gone
berserk! Also, it has strong political overtones in
that it involves the only federal judge in
America to have been born in Germany, and

spent his formative years under the Third Reich, and had been a Hitler Youth. I would be happy to mail you a copy of the book if you are interested, or know of persons who might be. Best regards, Jim Green
http://www.amazon.com/James-L.-Jim-Green/e/B001KHZIMM/ref=ntt_dp_epwbk_0

~

Fixing our unemployment crisis will do more to end gun violence in America—than any other legislation—So why does the Senate not include deficit neutral The Neighbor-To-Neighbor Job Creation Act: A federally mandated mutual insurance, owned by our employed, to provide a job to hire/train our unemployed? 86% of Americans support this—See ECONOMIC INCLUSIVISM, on Amazon/Kindle

~

FLIP-A-DISTRICT: Dist 21, TX—also, Real Time 2/28/14—Bill: Austin Goolsbee did not answer your question—you asked should we do something because work is disappearing—and he gave you the usual BS—rather than acknowledging that unemployment is a "social" problem—we as a society have the RESPONSIBILITY to address. See: FULL EMPLOYMENT IS A PRO-MARKET CONCEPT, Amazon/Kindle—YouTube: JGREEN56789

~

FLIP-A-DISTRICT—in 2000 I ran against Rep. Lamar Smith, Dist 21, TX—the man is an idiot….is set to Chair House Science Committee—says man has nothing to do with climate change--http://www.amazon.com/James-L.-Jim-Green/e/B001KHZIMM/ref=ntt_dp_epwbk_0

~

A question for Issa, EVERY Republican "Do you believe the market can provide anybody wanting a job, with a job"? Issa's et al belief in this fairytale is the reason we have 12 million unemployed in America.
http://www.amazon.com/James-L.-Jim-Green/e/B001KHZIMM/ref=ntt_dp_epwbk_0

~

Labor Day Question: What is preventing us from solving our unemployment crisis? FULL EMPLOYMENT IS A PRO-MARKET CONCEPT/Kindle--it is common sense--the majority of Americans support full employment--so why do we have 12 million jobless Americans? The reason is not for a lack of money, or jobs, but rather from a lack of imagination—

~

REGARDING SYRIA: I see a cartoon—with the "coalition" of nations in support of a retaliatory strike huddled together—pointing a finger at Uncle Sam—with the caption "You do it"....
http://www.amazon.com/James-L.-Jim-Green/e/B001KHZIMM/ref=ntt_dp_epwbk_0

~

Half the Republicans hate President Obama because they are racists, and the other half because he "won"—Since Roosevelt, the Republicans have had childish temper tantrums if the Democrats won, and they spew out false, vitriolic blather—[Limbaugh, FOX, etc.]--While [most] Democrats speak from fact-based

truths—Republicans hold facts and the truth in contempt! FACT: Reagan was the worst president in American history, until Bush II bumped him out of last place....
OUR GREED AND IGNORANCE, on Amazon/Kindle

~

Has anyone heard the latest FOX/REPUBLICAN scenario on Benghazi....President Obama and Hillary sneaked into Benghazi...in the dark of night....carrying a Bazooka...can the Republicans get any nuttier? The problem with repeating this lunacy [common fodder on right-wing-nut media] is that they have followers dumb enough to believe it! THERE IS NO BENGHAZI SCANDAL-- PERIOD! See: OUR GREED AND IGNORANCE, on Amazon/Kindle

~

Here is what happened re flight 370: The plane was hi-jacked—to shake off the hi-jackers the pilot[s] took the plane to 48,000 feet and then went into a steep dive—and in the stress on the descent the plane came apart and sadly is at the bottom of the Bay of Bengal. Reader: Your theory?

~

Have the Republicans gone nuts? Sticking it to our farmers! Who do they think is the beneficiary of the $40 billion they cut from FOOD STAMPS [gutting the program] so they can teach those moochers [hungry children] a lesson! Only persons with deep-seated feelings of inferiority could support the mind-set of the radical Republicans in Congress, today! http://www.amazon.com/James-L.-Jim-Green/e/B001KHZIMM/ref=ntt_dp_epwbk_0

~

The Democrats should play Billy Preston's "Nothing From Nothing is Nothing" at the Republican's bogus hearing on Benghazi --If the Republicans were really concerned about "our four dead Americans"—they would profusely apologize for cutting funds for security, they would spend the money wasted—tracking down the perpetrators, and they would stop dancing on their graves—to raise money! OUR GREED AND IGNORANCE, Amazon

~

Bill Maher: Your guest 5/9/14 who railed against President Obama for the deficit—omitted one big fact! Our current deficit is the price tag for saving our economy, after Supply-Side insanity trashed it! And Baker under Reagan did the exact same thing in 1987! Supply-Side has a shelf-life of 7 years before the economy collapses! And our deficit was only $60 billion in 1980, when Reagan took office--before neo-liberalism! OUR GREED AND IGNORANCE, Amazon

~

THE TRUTH: Ginning up the lunacy of the Republicans in DC, and their bogus hearing[s]...are their racist rank and file who are desperate to de-legitimatize President Obama [because he is black]—So when you hear FOX/Republicans uttering this total nonsense about Benghazi, etc., folks, they are talking to these people! See: IT IS IMPOSSIBLE TO BE A CHRISTIAN, AND VOTE REPUBLICAN, on Amazon/Kindle

~

THE POLLS ON OBAMACARE ARE DISHONEST! Where is the poll on Obamacare that excludes those who get their "news" from Fox, etc., and another factor in honest polling is to evaluate how many of those who speak negatively about Obamacare—understand the "for profit" system we [partially] replaced? http://www.amazon.com/James-L.-Jim-Green/e/B001KHZIMM/ref=ntt_dp_epwbk_0

~

I don't get Kentucky….they have a really great Democrat governor….and two absolute creeps—both Republicans, for U.S. Senators—with McConnell being the worst U.S. Senator in American history, until Rand Paul came along and bumped him out of last place—and why anyone would vote for McConnell escapes me! See: **IT IS IMPOSSIBLE TO BE A CHRISTIAN, AND VOTE REPUBLICAN**, on Amazon/Kindle

~

Like millions of Americans, I abhor the Republican's singular agenda: To use the American people as a battering ram to undermine President Obama—Stand up for America, and the American people this November: Throw the BUMS out—VOTE DEMOCRAT! See: OUR GREED AND IGNORANCE, on Amazon/Kindle

~

How to identify a racist:
1] They think Hawaii is a foreign country.
2] They think President Obama is a Muslim.
3] They tell you it is his policies, not his race they are opposed to [the Prez is center right]—.
4] If they oppose a Bill, the minute the Prez supports it—They are a racist—[add to, and pass it on]--
http://www.amazon.com/James-L.-Jim-Green/e/B001KHZIMM/ref=ntt_dp_epwbk_0

~

If the Republican/Tea Party had their way we wouldn't even have a U.S. Department of Veterans Affairs—You know….. "smaller government" which is code for "so our billionaires don't have to pay any taxes"—it makes you wonder how long will it take the Republican rank and file to catch on? To "get it" that they have been duped by Republican propaganda—and give Faux the finger? See OUR GREED AND IGNORANCE, Amazon

~

CNN RE the LA shooting….Why do you keep talking about the police and mental health system….RATHER than the real culprits---Wayne LaPierre, and his evil meanderings, and the NRA membership for not speaking out, and the Republicans in Congress—who obstructed and turned their back on the parents at Sandy Hook—which could have prevented this crime! IT IS IMPOSSIBLE TO BE A CHRISTIAN, AND VOTE REPUBLICAN, Amazon

~

We have 5% of the world's population, and 25% of all inmates on earth in our prisons! We now spend more locking people up, than we spend on educating our youth—We have the same prison population as China, but they have a billion more people—GET THE PICTURE—The "loud music" racist is going to prison for life—GOOD—so why would we take money from our youth's education, and punish taxpayers—by prolonging?

See: OUR GREED AND IGNORANCE, on Amazon/Kindle

~

If the Republican/Tea Party [hereafter RATP] Hate Big Government—it means they hate Americans-- BECAUSE in America THE GOVERNMENT IS THE PEOPLE! [maybe they just hate themselves]—The Result: America is moving in one direction—and RATP is moving in another!
http://www.amazon.com/.../e/B001KHZIMM/ref=ntt_dp_epwbk_0

~

In the law there is a term "prima facie"—i.e. when something is evident on its face—and the most recent prima facie criminal offense by Roberts and the four midgets, on our "Supreme Court"—to hand a blank check to our billionaires to buy our elections—is so blatantly criminal WE should have locked these jerks up and thrown the key away after Citizens United! See: OUR GREED AND IGNORANCE, on Amazon/Kindle

~

Issa said "It will be President Obama's fault if the government shuts down"....i.e., if he doesn't cave into the Republican kidnap for ransom list—it will be his fault! In short, Issa is saying his vote will be a "look what you made me do" [This is how psychopaths think!]....WHY IS OUR MEDIA NOT HOLDING THIS AH ACCOUNTABLE?
http://www.amazon.com/James-L.-Jim-Green/e/B001KHZIMM/ref=ntt_dp_epwbk_0

~

A recent poll found a 100% correlation between our racists, AND those suffering from "Benghazitis"—i.e., a racist malady--If the Republicans were really concerned about "our four dead Americans"—they would profusely apologize for cutting funds for security, they would spend the money wasted—tracking down the perpetrators, and they would stop dancing on their graves—to raise money! OUR GREED AND IGNORANCE, Amazon

~

It is leaking out that the Republicans in Congress who voted against background checks did so to pander to their racist constituents who—in their ignorance and hatred of blacks—i.e., would see a Yes vote as support for President Obama's leadership—which these racists want to undermine! Is this nuts or what? See: OUR GREED AND IGNORANCE, Amazon/Kindle

~

Anyone who would "volunteer" to defend America, at the risk of his own life is BRAVE...so let's dispense with the right-wing garbage—[who are currently spending millions to trash Bergdahl]—and to walk into an area where Americans are shot on sight is either incredibly brave, or crazy—take your pick. And Gitmo will be closed in less than 6mos—so why not get something out of it? IT IS IMPOSSIBLE TO BE A CHRISTIAN, AND VOTE REPUBLICAN, Amazon

~

The pernicious enemy of "public-sector" jobs is the archaic BELIEF that the market can provide anybody wanting a job, with a job—but this hasn't true since the mid-1970's—and due to automation, alone, is less and less true as we advance into the 21st Century…86% of Americans believe "anybody willing to work should be able to find a job". FULL EMPLOYMENT IS A PRO-MARKET CONCEPT, on Amazon/Kindle

~

FAUX is a propaganda channel--for our radical extremists who want to relegate America to the 8th Century—BC—think of FAUX as an American Taliban, with a mic—in short, you cannot trust a word they say--the same as the Taliban—for instance, FAUX…will not tell—in trashing Bergdahl--the Taliban have killed thousands more Afghans, than Americans, ad nauseam. See: OUR GREED AND IGNORANCE, Amazon

~

It is inconceivable that Speaker Boehner does not see as intrinsically wrong that the American taxpayer is subsidizing the oil industry to the tune of $5 billion—while they are they are making the highest profits in history—and soaking the American taxpayer at the pump— And yet the Republicans in Congress refuse to revise the Tax Code, and Boehner keeps saying

"President Obama got his tax increase in January"—See: OUR GREED AND IGNORANCE, Amazon

~

It is mind shattering—the absence of subtlety—from our one and only foreign-born terrorist, Ted Cruz, and I'll paraphrase—"If Obamacare goes into affect...it will be widely accepted by the American people—and we Republicans will never be able to get rid of it". And this is a justification to trash the ACA? IT IS IMPOSSIBLE TO BE A CHRISTIAN AND VOTE REPUBLICAN, Amazon

~

Joe-MSNBC...Why did no one ask Thune if he believes "The market can provide anybody wanting a job, with a job"—You see...it is because Thune [every Republican] REALLY believes this FALSE statement that causes him to blather on about imaginary jobs Republicans are going to create—IT IS BS—This BELIEF cost us 10.1 million jobs in the meltdown! See: FULL EMPLOYMENT IS A PRO-MARKET CONCEPT, on Amazon/Kindle

~

Joe, on Morning Joe....just as I am about to think you are not one of the nutty Republicans—you know, the "not decent" fascists who have taken over the party, Cruz, Paul, Ryan, et al—and you come up with a goofy comment—hoping the Supreme Court will "knock down a pillar of Obamacare"—you want to deprive women of contraception? HAVE YOU GONE NUTS! See: OUR GREED AND IGNORANCE, Amazon

~

Charlie Rose--FACE THE NATION: Lillian Hellman's book about scoundrels during the McCarthy era..."Scoundrel Time"....Are back, i.e., the speakers at Republican's CPAC, complete with a carbon copy of McCarthy—Ted Cruz—in short, These are NOT DECENT PEOPLE—decent people do not advocate for an America unfit for human habitation! So why doesn't our media call them what they are—JERKS/SCOUNDRELS? Bio: http://www.amazon.com/James-L.-Jim-Green/e/B001KHZIMM/ref=ntt_dp_epwbk_0

~

It is difficult to determine whether we should be more concerned with the Russians, or the Republicans! With Putin's wild west aggression on a sovereign nation, the Republicans are undermining President Obama's efforts to mitigate this powder keg! It is no secret that the Republican vitriolic blather is to appeal to their racists—but this undermines America! See: OUR GREED AND IGNORANCE, on Amazon/Kindle

~

MEDIA FOLK: The "C" in Conservative has come to stand for "Crazy"[and Cruz], and the "R" in Republican has come to stand for "Racists"—So there you have it—America is under attack from CRAZY RACISTS—[and the Koch Bros are Nazis]--and this bunch poses a far greater threat to America, than TERRORISM!
http://www.amazon.com/James-L.-Jim-Green/e/B001KHZIMM/ref=ntt_dp_epwbk_0

~

MEDIA FOLK: Why are you letting Ryan, any of these Republican lunatics, to get away with

ANY semblance of piety on our DEBT—WHEN THEY DROVE US INTO A $10 TRILLION DITCH, SENDING OUR ECONOMY INTO MELTDOWN?
http://www.amazon.com/James-L.-Jim-Green/e/B001KHZIMM/ref=ntt_dp_epwbk_0

~

MEDIA: Ted Cruz is no Hispanic….and no offense to Canada…but Cruz denouncing his Canadian citizenship has cut off only one more opportunity for us Americans to get rid of this grandstanding buffoon….McCarthy-imitator—who panders to our bottom-feeders, ignorant and our racists to gin up support…So Ignore Him! See: OUR GREED AND IGNORANCE, on Amazon/Kindle

~

MEDIA: Why are we wasting so much of our time on push-back from the current crop of Republicans—who want an America with both feet planted in the 8th Century, BC? For instance, why would anyone hand a mic to Blackburn in Tennessee—she blathers on with Republican lunacy for the benefit of our racists—while the vast majority of Americans are moving in another direction…See: OUR GREED AND IGNORANCE, on Amazon

~

We can't fix an engine, absent the correct tools to fix it…a metaphor specific to our JOB CREATION IN AMERICA: We shift from one foot to the other--waiting on the Market to create jobs it is INCAPABLE of creating, has been incapable since the mid-1970's—and given automation, alone—becomes less capable in the 21st Century! It is SPECIOUS to speak of job creation—absent the correct tool to fix it! OUR GREED AND IGNORANCE, Amazon

~

MEDIA: WHY do we persist in undermining our economy—by leaving our "job creation" up to the market, in the 21st Century? The market has been INCAPABLE of providing everybody wanting a job, with a job, since the mid-1970's! We are on an everyone loses path! People do not buy the products manufactured for the market—WHEN THEY ARE UNEMPLOYED! FULL EMPLOYMENT IS A PRO-MARKET CONCEPT, on Amazon/Kindle

~

Morley Safer—re NEW YORKER cartoons—
please see the one included in a Petition to the
U.S. Supreme Court—Docket #79-1627—in the
archives to this day--the caption reads
"Excellent, excellent, a fine blend of truth, half-
truths, and blatant falsehoods"—a reprint in
THE HARVARD BOYS CLUB, Amazon, will
explain the reason, and relevance.

~

Morning Joe—Joe….I know you are a
Republican…but thought you had some
sense….until you spoke highly of Cheney this
morning….and that showed you to be as crazy
as the House lunatics! We don't celebrate odious
toads in America….Cheney is not a decent
person—and has done more harm to America
than any other person in our history!
http://www.amazon.com/James-L.-Jim-
Green/e/B001KHZIMM/ref=ntt_dp_epwbk_0

~

MSNBC – JANSING—A challenge—ask "so
called" economic expert Peter Morici if he
believes "The market can provide anybody

wanting a job, with a job" $100 says Morici [every Republican] BELIEVES this to his toes— and yet, given automation, alone, this hasn't been true since the mid-1970's—with high joblessness in all of the OECD countries, since! See: FULL EMPLOYMENT IS A PRO-MARKET CONCEPT, Amazon/Kindle

~

SUPER COMMITTEE NEW RULE: Paul Ryan doesn't get to claim to be this great champion of deficit reduction—UNTIL HE PROFUSELY APOLOGIZES TO THE AMERICAN PEOPLE FOR VOTING TO ADD $7 TRILLION TO OUR DEFICIT UNDER BUSH—And ditto to all of the hypocrites in the Republican Tea Party! http://pac.petitions.moveon.org/sign/recall-ted-cruz-immediately

~

NEW RULE: This is a test [MSNBC, et al] to determine the % of Republicans who are racists....Every Republican guest must cite one positive accomplishment by President Obama-- BEFORE they are permitted to go off on their vitriolic rant to appease the racists back home—

if they are unable to cite even one—THEY ARE A RACIST!
http://pac.petitions.moveon.org/sign/recall-ted-cruz-immediately

~

Our climate change-deniers have two parents: GREED and JOBS—GREED on the part of the 1%, who want to drill the Rockies down to an anthill for pure selfishness [and at the expense of the planet]; and those in the 99%, who in their ignorance, believe that if we block the 1%--they won't have a JOB—The planet be dam—d! See: OUR GREED AND IGNORANCE, on Amazon/Kindle

~

THE REPUBLICAN BUFFONS ON BEHGHAZI IS NONSENSE! The mistake Democrats make is that they try to give rational answers to irrational Republican questions! If the Republicans are wringing their hands over "security"—WHY DID THEY CUT THE FUNDING FOR SECURITY? IT IS IMPOSSIBLE TO BE A CHRISTIAN, AND VOTE REPUBLICAN, on Amazon/Kindle

~

The most dangerous BELIEF in America, today, is: "The market can provide anybody wanting a job, with a job"—this is patently false, and given "automation", alone, this BELIEF becomes more and more pernicious with each passing year—and our clinging to this BELIEF is the reason we have 12 million jobless, in America. For the solution see: FULL EMPLOYMENT IS A PRO-MARKET CONCEPT, Amazon/Kindle

~

Our mainstream media is asleep—ALEC, staffed with Donald Sagretti imitators—and bouncing out laws determined to relegate America back to the 8th Century such as "stand your ground", and "gay law" in Arizona--Where is the expose? Bring these JERKS out into the daylight! See:
http://www.amazon.com/James-L.-Jim-Green/e/B001KHZIMM/ref=ntt_dp_epwbk_0

~

CNN Your Money—Given automation, alone, our market economy can no longer function without public-sector jobs. FULL

EMPLOYMENT IS A PRO-MARKET CONCEPT, Amazon

~

Our pundits struggle to define the slimeballs who have taken over the Republican Party—a thoughtful definition is "Regressive"—but that is too kind—McConnell, Paul, Cruz, Ryan, et al, are NOT DECENT PEOPLE….decent people don't act/talk like that—and their trash talk about President Obama is to our lowest common denominator—OUR RACISTS— http://www.amazon.com/James-L.-Jim-Green/e/B001KHZIMM/ref=ntt_dp_epwbk_0

~

THE SOURCE OF OUR HYPER-PARTISANSHIP: The Republicans in Congress are trying to destroy America, i.e., the American economy—injuring millions of Americans in the process--so they can pander to, and count on, their racist constituents in the next election [who are driven by their hatred of President Obama]—It is driven by RACISM! See: OUR GREED AND IGNORANCE, on Amazon/Kindle

~

Why aren't we honest about this? The FUEL driving the hyper-partisanship that has Washington in paralysis is: RACISM! In his press conference on 4/30/13 President Obama said re Republicans in Congress "compromising with me [a black man] is a betrayal"—SURE, WITH RACISTS! So is America doomed by "OUR GREED AND IGNORANCE", on Amazon/Kindle?

~

3/7/14 Jobs Report--MOST of our "so called" economic experts BELIEVE, REALLY BELIEVE: "The market can provide anybody wanting a job, with a job"—it is BS, hasn't been true since the mid-1970's, and given automation, alone, is even less true in the 21st Century! But this 8th Century BELIEF persists, at the expense of the jobless, and the Market! FULL EMPLOYMENT IS A PRO-MARKET CONCEPT, Amazon/Kindle
http://www.amazon.com/James-L.-Jim-Green/e/B001KHZIMM/ref=ntt_dp_epwbk_0

~

Chuck Todd—Daily Rundown....This woman Rep from Tennessee, Blackburn or something like that, is an IDIOT! Why did you pick her....What she is going to say is predictable....she just blathers on with glittering generalities and Republican hogwash—and she is INDIFFERENT to the truth!
http://www.amazon.com/James-L.-Jim-Green/e/B001KHZIMM/ref=ntt_dp_epwbk_0

~

MEDIA--CHALLENGE OF THE DAY:
Finding a Republican, who:
1] Does not have a reckless disregard for the TRUTH!
2] Can put a sentence together without glittering generalities!
3] Will not blather on with Republican hogwash!
4] Speaks about what is good for America and Americans!
http://www.amazon.com/James-L.-Jim-Green/e/B001KHZIMM/ref=ntt_dp_epwbk_0

~

Chris Matthews: Why did you say Cruz is "smart"—HE IS DANGEROUS--that is like saying McCarthy was smart…A demagogue's hubris and arrogance isn't smart—and he and his ilk, both incite and speak to/for our ignorant and racists—our lowest common denominator—We are not going to take America back from these clowns by calling them "smart"…. http://pac.petitions.moveon.org/sign/recall-ted-cruz-immediately

~

Regarding our recent racist outbursts—Racism has but a single parent—IGNORANCE---making general statements across ANY group because of their race is as IGNORANT as saying all women are short, and all men are tall—Now if the Republicans will just target our racists in their voter fraud crusade~~~[don't hold your breath, folks] See: OUR GREED AND IGNORANCE, on Amazon/Kindle

~

Rand Paul, looks like, acts like and talks like a Weasel—in short, and like virtually every Republican in Washington, today: NOT A DECENT PERSON—but, except for the tiny handful of persons of like kind—who on earth could possible see Paul as having presidential stature in America? See: IT IS IMPOSSIBLE TO BE A CHRISTIAN, AND VOTE REPUBLICAN, on Amazon/Kindle

~

RE House Republicans: IN YOUR GUTS, YOU KNOW THEY'RE NUTS!

~

Let's face it—the president dropped the ball...and it is his fault these Americans died....Oh, you thought I meant Benghazi---the reference is to Reagan and the 241 American troops who died in Beruit, and to Bush and the 3000 who died on 9-11.....Get it looney-toons? IT IS IMPOSSIBLE TO BE A CHRISTIAN, AND VOTE REPUBLICAN, Amazon

~

RE the trio, et al—Paul/Ryan/Cruz, etc., It is obvious that the Republican propaganda strategy in this election year is to throw "red meat" to their racists—but how wide [or more accurate, narrow] is this faction—and what percent of the electorate is being turned off by their hate language? OUR GREED AND IGNORANCE, Amazon

~

REPUBLICAN FRAUD--They claim if we cut taxes for the 1%, and cut regulations so corporations can cut corners [and make unsafe products at a lower cost and higher profits—i.e., based on pure GREED—their TRUE agenda]....But out of this deception they claim if we do this jobs will magically appear like moonbeams—it is not only a FRAUD, it is a FAIRY TALE, a CRUEL HOAX perpetrated on the American people. OUR GREED AND IGNORANCE, Amazon

~

Republicans/Faux need to get honest [but don't hold your breath]...they would condemn President Obama if he cured them of cancer! We have been making prisoner exchanges since the Civil War--And the bottom line is that we didn't abandon a soldier—a promise far more important than MORE "Republican Red Herring Nonsense"! OUR GREED AND IGNORNACE: Poses A Far Greater Danger To America, Than Terrorism, Amazon

~

The Republican attack on the ACA, Social Security, Medicare INSURANCE, etc. [Ryan's Budget, et al] is downright depraved! Like our auto insurance we chip in collectively—to protect us individually—The 1% doesn't pay for it---WE PAY FOR IT INDIVIDUALLY-- it is democracy at its finest! So why do Republicans call it "socialism"? BECAUSE THEY ARE IDIOTS!
IT IS IMPOSSIBLE TO BE A CHRISTIAN, AND VOTE REPUBLICAN, Amazon

~

"There is greater disparity between the rich and the poor today than there has ever been before."—sound familiar…it was written by Peter Drucker almost 50 years ago, but rather than fixing the social demise since: Citizens United, the Koch Bros "Greed for the sake of Greed", and Republican policies have doubled down—and put this disparity on steroids! IT IS IMPOSSIBLE TO BE A CHRISTIAN, AND VOTE REPUBLICAN, Amazon

~

The lesson to be taken from "CAPITAL in the Twenty-First Century" is that every economic theory currently relied on needs to be thrown out, EXCEPT those which acknowledge that an expanding and contracting public workforce [authorized in Public Law 15 USC § 3101] is an INDISPENSABLE component in the EFFECTIVE functioning of a modern market economy. See: FULL EMPLOYMENT IS A PRO-MARKET CONCEPT, Amazon

~

Rick Perry, a "star" in the now radical extremists
Republican Party [and their CPAC fringe]—is denying healthcare to millions of children in Texas, so he can make a racist statement against President Obama---So why is our media not asking of Perry and like Republican governors "WHAT KIND OF PEOPLE ARE THESE"? They are a disgrace to humankind! See: OUR GREED AND IGNORANCE, Amazon/Kindle

~

Should we pool our money to create a better society—Well, yes....

~

Show me a person who wants to impeach President Obama—and I'll show you a Racist! See: **IT IS IMPOSSIBLE TO BE A CHRISTIAN, AND VOTE REPUBLICAN, on Amazon/Kindle** http://www.amazon.com/James-L.-Jim-Green/e/B001KHZIMM/ref=ntt_dp_epwbk_0

~

Social Media, our new way of communicating, is a mixed blessing—on the one side, we meet wonderful and bright people we might otherwise never meet—the downside is the xenophobic "chopped liver for brains" crowd, all parroting the same Republican talking points—and spewing out this blithering lunacy—some so dumb they actually believe there is something to Benghazi—See: **OUR GREED AND IGNORANCE, on Amazon**

~

If the Republicans were really concerned about Benghazi—they would be profusely apologizing to the American people because they cut funding for Security at Benghazi—rather they are exploiting this tragedy to get blood money by selling t-shirts & coffee mugs to our ignorant who are so dumb they actually think FOX, is in the "News" business! See: IT IS IMPOSSIBLE TO BE A CHRISTIAN, AND VOTE REPUBLICAN, Amazon

~

The Democrats in the House should boycott this "monkey court" the Republicans want to waste our taxpayer money on—save for one member—perhaps on a rotating basis—someone outraged by this Republican nonsense—If the Republicans were really concerned about Benghazi—they would be profusely apologizing to the American people because they cut funding for Security at Benghazi! See: OUR GREED AND IGNORANCE, on Amazon

~

State of the Union: America is divided between the rich, and the poor, but evolving. SOTU: Is in a divisive struggle over whether to go forward into the 21st Century----or return to the 8th Century, BC [Huckabee, Paul, et al]!

http://www.amazon.com/James-L.-Jim-Green/e/B001KHZIMM/ref=ntt_dp_epwbk_0

~

Steve....UP....MSNBC....You had a Republican ideologue [RNC staff] on this AM, and you, your panel didn't ask him "Are Republicans petrified that the ACA will work, not that it won't?" Why is every Republican not being asked this question—after all, the Republicans tried to sabotage Social Security Insurance in 1935, for the same reason!
http://pac.petitions.moveon.org/sign/recall-ted-cruz-immediately

~

Doesn't it strike anyone as peculiar why the Republicans hate Social Security Insurance? Like all insurance, WE, the American people are pooling our money—It is OUR money, not THEIR money--Do they resent not having their hand in the till? Do the Republicans hate us Americans, like when they voted to gut Food Stamps? See: OUR GREED AND IGNORANCE, on Amazon

~

The federal judiciary is that thin black line that stands between our freedoms in America and a tyrannical dictatorship. The historical role of the federal courts is to be the "guardian" of our constitutional rights--but what if a federal judge, a former "Hitler Youth", falsified a court record with the INTENT to undermine our Constitution—See: THE HARVARD BOYS CLUB, on Amazon/Kindle [a true story]

~

For over 35 years I have relentlessly demanded the exposure of FRAUD by a Federal Judge INTENT on aborting legal rights of citizenship, the same as Hitler in 1938—even disregarding that the judge was a Hitler Youth—Without constitutional freedoms, we cease to be a free country—and in reality, Hitler has undermined the U.S. Constitution from his grave! See: THE HARVARD BOYS CLUB, on Amazon/Kindle

~

The biggest challenge facing America, today, is how do we fix it so we never again fall hostage to a miniscule handful of racist, Republican lunatics—who pose far more of a threat to

America than terrorism--fact and truth deniers, who in a temper tantrum, and unintelligible kidnap for ransom demands--threaten to burn America and our economy down! http://pac.petitions.moveon.org/sign/recall-ted-cruz-immediately

~

The common thread running through all of our current protests [Turkey, Occupy, Arab Spring] is a failure to acknowledge the human right to be a productive human being—and our failure to make it a "legal right"—and the policies in the OECD countries, including the US, are notorious for: Fix the Market, and this will fix Unemployment, when our policy should be exactly the opposite--See: A POOL OF SLAVES, on Amazon/Kindle

~

The division in America, today, is between "critical thinkers", and "literal thinkers" and if we could magically transform the later, into the former—the "Tea Party" [AKA Republican base]—with their bizarre notions about evolution, women's rights, and climate change [they don't understand the science on any]—the

"Tea Party" would disappear, overnight! See: OUR GREED AND IGNORANCE, Amazon

~

Our market recovery has gotten most of it right...we got it wrong when we said "me too" to the Republican "job creation model"—cut taxes for the 1%, and jobs will rain do like moonbeams --it is BS—a fairytale--the 1% bought bigger yachts with the extra cash—and gave the finger to the 11 million jobless! So, when Boehner says Republicans are "job creators"—HE'S LYING! OUR GREED AND IGNORANCE, Amazon

~

The only people who are voting Republican, today, are Blithering Idiots—OK, to walk that back—the Republican politicians do not make statements which make them sound like blithering idiots—and their current crop of extremists are making plenty of them [such a Rubio denying man-made climate change] -- UNLESS they are seeking votes from a Blithering Idiot...Capiche? See: OUR GREED AND IGNORANCE, on Amazon/Kindle

~

The plus side to the "End Times"—is that it will get rid of Michelle Bachmann— http://pac.petitions.moveon.org/sign/recall-ted-cruz-immediately

~

The Republi-Faux clowns, are like the little boy who cried wolf—waiving and flailing in a truth-challenged desperation for a non-existent "scandal"—to appease our racists in America—and would smear President Obama if he cured them of cancer—claiming he is up to the same Tricky-Dicky agenda they are notorious for—In short, if their lips are moving, they are lying! OUR GREED AND IGNORANCE, Amazon

~

The Republicans are saying that it never occurred to terrorists to kidnap for trade before---REALLY? And if anyone believes this Republican CLAPTRAP—there is a bridge in Brooklyn…..Bla, Bla, Bla—IT IS IMPOSSIBLE TO BE A CHRISTIAN, AND VOTE REPUBLICAN, on Amazon/Kindle

~

Limbaugh's retort to Pope Francis re the evils of "trickle down" is very telling—Limbaugh said it was "puzzling"—i.e., Limbaugh BELIEVES the market can provide everyone with a job—BUT THIS HASN'T BEEN TRUE SINCE THE MID-1970's. In short, the Republican agenda is a MENACE to capitalism, and the sooner the Democrats nail them on their FRAUD, the better! FULL EMPLOYMENT IS PRO-MARKET CONCEPT, Amazon/Kindle

~

The Republican candidates for congress/president have been bought and paid for by the Koch bros....they are not decent people....decent people do not talk, or advocate what Cruz, Paul, Cantor, Ryan, Perry et al do— the whole lot of them are creeps—and it hangs like a dark cloud over the Republican party. See: IT IS IMPOSSIBLE TO BE A CHRISTIAN, AND VOTE REPUBLICAN, on Amazon/Kindle

~

What is wrong in the House—is that the racist Republican Tea Party voted in racist candidates—with a County Commissioner mind-set—persons who are incapable of critical thinking—who are in way over their head, and think macroeconomics is about fixing potholes on a county road—in a word: IDIOTS!
http://pac.petitions.moveon.org/sign/recall-ted-cruz-immediately

~

WE, the American people are the "government" per Lincoln…i.e., the "government" is buying the products of capitalism….further, absent our collectively infusing cash into our economy for the betterment of America—capitalism would collapse in a New York Second…So why do Republicans, today, have such contempt for "government"—BECAUSE THEY ARE IDIOTS!
See: OUR GREED AND IGNORANCE, on Amazon/Kindle

~

Toure—MSNBC The Cycle [6/14/13]—regarding the federal judge you quoted, William W Schwarzer, re the war on drugs—you need to be made aware that he was a Hitler Youth—and falsified a federal court record with the SPECIFIC INTENT to undermine the U.S. Constitution—hardly consistent with your quote...See: THE HARVARD BOYS CLUB, on Amazon/Kindle

Jim Green, Demo candidate for Congress, 2000

~

TO: The black-hearted, mean-spirited, anti-Christian REPUBLICANS [and most likely racists] in the 24 states who are blocking expansion of the ACA in their state—and injuring millions of American children in the process—I have a book for you: IT IS IMPOSSIBLE TO BE A CHRISTIAN, AND VOTE REPUBLICAN, on Amazon/Kindle; again, IT IS IMPOSSIBLE TO BE A CHRISTIAN, AND VOTE REPUBLICAN— Get it?

~

We have the "legal authority" in America to limit our unemployment to "3%"--but "0" plans on the table to make it a reality—and we need to drill down on why do we do this [maybe the oligarchy want Americans with minimal rights

as employees—you think?]--Jobs beget jobs—
"private-sector jobs"—SO why on earth do we
persist on going down a path that undermines
the very thing we are trying to create—a strong
and viable market? FULL EMPLOYMENT IS
A PRO-MARKET CONCEPT, on
Amazon/Kindle

~

We should never condemn the CEO who closes a
plant, when they is losing money—but we should
be outraged by a Republican House that is
incapable or unwilling to address the "social"
problems caused by the loss of jobs! FULL
EMPLOYMENT IS A PRO-MARKET
CONCEPT, Amazon

~

The Republican hysteria over the ACA is real—
THEY ARE PETRIFIED THAT IT WILL
SUCCEED....and Cruz/OReiley et al waving
and flailing about is a CONTRIVED talking
point—FOX [the shameless liars] daily have
people telling of having lost their car, and house,
and dog—because of the ACA—WHICH
DOESN'T GO INTO EFFECT UNTIL
JANUARY!

~

Climate Change-deniers in the rank and file is because they believe that unless we let the 1% drill the Rockies down to an anthill [for pure GREED]—they won't be able to get a JOB—the most pernicious belief today is "The market can provide anybody wanting a job, with a job"—it is FALSE—and the above is the fall-out. Re: OUR GREED AND IGNORANCE, on Amazon

~

The Republican /Tea Party has become the "Miserable excuse for a human being party"— for instance, they set as a PRIORITY, again PRIORITY—to cut $40 billion [to gut] Food Stamps—with most of the food going to feed children—so they could give the $40 billion TO GREEDY BILLIONAIRES! To be a Christian, one must follow his teachings, thus: IT IS IMPOSSIBLE TO BE A CHRISTIAN, AND VOTE REPUBLICAN, Amazon/Kindle

~

The Republican party has moved so far to the radical right [there are NO moderate Republicans, today]—that the "C" in Conservative, their favorite identity, has come to stand for "Crackpot", "Crazy", "Certifiable" take your pick—and all we need ad is Michelle Bachmann, to complete the picture—and they stand for everything Jesus spoke out against—thus: IT IS IMPOSSIBLE TO A CHRISTIAN, AND VOTE REPUBLICAN, Amazon

~

THE REPUBLICAN PARTY IN A NUTSHELL, TODAY: The Republicans want to trash America--as their means to trash President Obama--so they can please their racist constituents. OUR GREED AND IGNORANCE, Amazon

~

The Republican Party should change it name to the non sequitur party—for the "rank and file", many of their solutions to do not even remotely follow the problem at hand—for instance, the talking point by Republicans in the House that gutting the Food Stamp program will lead to better nutrition----IT IS IMPOSSIBLE TO BE

A CHRISTIAN, AND VOTE REPUBLICAN,
Amazon

~

THE Republicans are IDIOTS for cutting
unemployment benefits—injuring the
unemployed, and at the same time throwing a
monkey wrench into our economy/recovery—in
short, THE REPUBLICANS ARE A MENACE
TO THE MARKET! And some [their racists]
are using the American people as a battering
ram to undermine President Obama—and
President Obama could count on them in
Bergdahl's release? GIVE US A BREAK! OUR
GREED AND IGNORANCE, on
Amazon/Kindle

~

The Republicans claim to want the same kind of
America the Democrats do—to build a good and
decent America....it is just that there is a little
chink in the method the Republicans use to get
there: For instance, their job creation is to let
the 1% drill the Rockies down to an anthill—
FOR PURE GREED—the Earth be dam—d--
and they promise the 1% will throw us 99%

bread crumbs, etc. OUR GREED AND IGNORANCE, Amazon

~

The tail wagging the dog in America, today, is a faction of the most ignorant humans—on the face of the earth....our racists! The Republicans in Congress, being the cowards they are, are beholden to our racists—McConnell even filibustered a bill, HE WROTE, once President Obama supported! See: OUR GREED AND IGNAORNACE, on Amazon/Kindle

~

The TSA's error with the 9 year old...is a microcosm of a larger problem with our system: WHY are we allowing a tiny handful of lunatics—who are moving in one direction— while the rest of the world is moving in another....TAKE THE LATTER HOSTAGE? http://www.amazon.com/James-L.-Jim-Green/e/B001KHZIMM/ref=ntt_dp_epwbk_0

~

The "C" for Dan Patrick [Republican candidate for Texas Lt. Governor]—does not stand for

"Conservative", but rather "Certifiable"—The upside for sane Americans, however, is that we now have an exact % of Republicans who are certified "Tea Party" voters [no pun intended]…i.e… 10%…and no sane woman in Texas will vote for Patrick in the general if they listen to his ramblings! IT IS IMPOSSIBLE TO BE A CHRISTIAN, AND VOTE REPUBLICAN, Amazon

~

Why do we have so many Americans who confuse "socialism" with "democracy"? It all started with the hysteria of McCarthyism—when our literal thinkers were waving and flailing in fear that we had a "commie" behind every tree.…Example: "86% of Americans believe that anybody wanting to work should be able to find a job" but the market is INCAPABLE of meeting the will of the American people, i.e., FULL EMPLOYMENT IS A PRO-MARKET CONCEPT, Amazon

~

Our "literal thinkers" are determined to sink America, and they would rather destroy our market economy than acknowledge that the market is INCAPABLE of providing enough jobs-and in spite of: "86% of Americans believe that anybody wanting to work should be able to find a job"—we are a democracy. OUR GREED AND IGNORANCE, Amazon

~

Ed: The CBO projects that on our current path it will be 2017 before we get back to even an anemic 5.5% unemployment rate--with unemployment benefits long since expired, and if the market fails, the jobless are out of luck! So why, on God's Earth, have we thrown our hands up and claim they are tied? We are the can-do nation—we don't have to put up with this—SO WHY DO WE? FULL EMPLOYMENT IS A PRO-MARKET CONCEPT, Amazon

~

"Conservative" has come to mean "Certifiable" in today's Republican party—and just when we think they can't get any crazier we hear that some believe Noah took dinosaurs with him on his ark [you can't make this up]—but what is down right scary is that we have a House filled with these "Conservative" lunatics who want to relegate America to the 8th Century, BC! IT IS

IMPOSSIBLE TO BE A CHRISTIAN, AND VOTE REPUBLICAN, Amazon

~

Better a "liberal", than a "literal"—Example: "86% of Americans believe that anybody wanting to work should be able to find a job"-- in the face of a market INCAPABLE of meeting the will of the American people—but our "literals" would rather destroy the market than change, i.e., more forward with: FULL EMPLOYMENT IS A PRO-MARKET CONCEPT, Amazon

~

The most pernicious belief in America, today, is: "The market can provide anybody wanting a job, with a job"—this has been less and less true since the mid-1970's, and given "automation", alone, is compounding exponentially—but we would rather destroy our market economy than give up this archaic belief! High Unemployment/Sluggish recovery is not a non-sequitur-- FULL EMPLOYMENT IS A PRO-MARKET CONCEPT, Amazon

~

The Republican obstructionism--so they can score political points with our racists, i.e., using the American people, and America as a battering ram to undermine President Obama, is despicable —but Boehner has it right, in our proclivity to fire people, in this case Skinseki, by asking "will this solve the problem?"…..and Why do we put firing like a loose cannon ahead of fixing our problems? See OUR GREED AND IGNORANCE, Amazon

~

Just when it was beginning to look like Republicans couldn't get any crazier [or creepier] than Ted Cruz--the Republican Convention in Texas took another radical step toward an America unfit for human habitation, by their platform! See: IT IS IMPOSSIBLE TO BE A CHRISTIAN, AND VOTE REPUBLICAN, Amazon

~

There is something seriously wrong—when a great country like America has allowed itself to fall prey to a tiny, tiny handful of the looniest fruit cakes on the face of the Earth [Michelle

Bachmann, AKA Tea Party]—and we need to seriously drill down on how we can PREVENT THIS FROM EVER HAPPENING AGAIN! http://www.amazon.com/James-L.-Jim-Green/e/B001KHZIMM/ref=ntt_dp_epwbk_0

~

How on Earth can a Republican Loonie, Like Paul Ryan claim to be a champion of deficit reduction—WHEN HE VOTED TO INCREASE OUR DEFICIT BY $7 TRILLION UNDER BUSH! Further, these Tea Party Loonies want to use INSURANCE payments by citizens for Social Security and Healthcare—TO BE SPENT ON WARS! THROW THE BUMS OUT! http://www.amazon.com/James-L.-Jim-Green/e/B001KHZIMM/ref=ntt_dp_epwbk_0

~

The Republican idea of a "Grand Bargain" is how they can cheat millions of Americans out of INSURANCE CLAIMS they have paid for years for Social Security, and now Healthcare—SO THEY CAN GIVE THIS ILLGOTTEN GAIN TO THE 1%! When on Earth will Red State

Republicans realize THEYARE BEING SHAFTED!
http://www.amazon.com/James-L.-Jim-Green/e/B001KHZIMM/ref=ntt_dp_epwbk_0

~

To explain the division that has America in gridlock, consider: We are divided by our "literal" vs "critical" thinkers—by claiming 24 hours, is 24 hours, by God—the former deny evolution, claim the Earth is 6000 years old, and Noah took dinosaurs with him on his ark [you can't make this up]— WE are a democracy, folks—this requires our having INFORMED VOTERS! See: OUR GREED AND IGNORANCE, Amazon

~

In switching back and forth between MSNBC and FAUX re President Obama's speech to West Point—We see an inspired vision for America on MSNBC—on FAUX we see a tearing down of America, and President Obama, in particular—this negativism on FAUX [Rove] may reinforce our naysayers, obstructers, and racists—but it does nothing re our working

together to solve our problems in America!
OUR GREED AND IGNORANCE, Amazon

~

A QUESTION FOR THE READER—this is a
one question survey—there is not a good or bad
answer, rather, what do you PERSONALLY
believe: A policy-driving pervasive belief, today,
is that: The Market can provide anybody
wanting a job, with a job—do you
PERSONALLY believe this?

~

To use a metaphor—Our economy is like a 747,
currently flying at 20,000 feet—and being brain-
damaged, the Republican/Tea Party, complying
with racists to undermine President Obama—
WANT TO CUT THE ENGINES! See: OUR
GREED AND IGNORANCE, Amazon

~

When on earth are we going to figure out: When
we deduct out those who hang on every word
from FOX, re our polls on Obamacare—it is
wildly popular.....AND, that every person in this
group is suffering from DEEP-SEATED

FEELINGS OF INFERIORITY—They can only feel tall, by looking upon those getting Food Stamps, etc., as small—SICK!
http://www.amazon.com/James-L.-Jim-Green/e/B001KHZIMM/ref=ntt_dp_epwbk_0

~

When on earth will someone in the media ask Rubio, et al—re their new-found religion about the poor—"WHAT IS YOUR SOLUTION"? You can bet the farm he will say "Cut taxes for the 1%, they will build factories with the windfall of cash, and every one will have a job in the factory"—Yes, folks it is the same old BS— been there, did that—it drove our economy into meltdown, and a 14..4 million job loss! See: FULL EMPLOYMENT IS A PRO-MARKET CONCEPT, Amazon

~

When we go to vote in America…it is to vote for someone who has our back—someone who is in our corner….and if you vote for any Republican for national office—and you are not the Koch Brothers—I have a bridge in Brooklyn to sell you….See: OUR GREED AND IGNORANCE

~

Whenever we hear Republican politicians talking crazy—such as Rubio denying climate change—it is because they are talking to constituents—who are equally as crazy! But, WHY on earth would the 99% be denying climate change? ANSWER: The 1% deny for PURE GREED—so they can drill the Rockies down to an anthill—BUT the 99% think this is their ONLY way to get a JOB—the Earth be dam—d! OUR GREED AND IGNORACE, Amazon

~

Where on earth did these creeps come from? This
crop of the most mean-spirited, loonies on the face of the earth—The Republicans in Congress—and consummate proof: They cut $40 billion from Food Stamps—injuring children, farmers, our economy—AND DEVOID OF COMMON DECENCY!
http://pac.petitions.moveon.org/sign/recall-ted-cruz-immediately

~

Dear Republicans in Congress: Economics 101—We can't siphon America's wealth away from the consuming middle—without sending our economy into meltdown [1987 & 2008]--YOU NITWITS! And then giving this ill gotten gain to the 1% for PURE GREED [your ONE and ONLY program]—is levying war against the American people—i.e., this is TREASON! http://pac.petitions.moveon.org/sign/recall-ted-cruz-immediately

~

Why ANYONE would vote Republican is a total mystery….the Republican party has been taken over by extremists who advocate for an America unfit for human habitation…..where bullies run roughshod over women and children, with impunity—and they support stealing from the poor, to give to the rich—the book title says it all IT IS IMPOSSIBLE TO BE A CHRISTIAN, AND VOTE REPUBLICAN, on Amazon/Kindle

~

QUESTION READ/ANSWERED BY ED-MSNBC: Why does our media treat unemployment with such indifference? We do not have ANY program SPECIFIC to ending unemployment! We are waiting on the market to solve this "social" problem—and if the market fails, the unemployed are out of luck! HINT: We are using the wrong model! High unemployment/ Sluggish recovery is not a non sequitur! FULL EMPLOYMENT IS A PRO-MARKET CONCEPT, on Amazon/Kindle

~

Unemployment causes problems. Serious personal problems, as well as serious "social" problems--
Why is "unemployment"—as a stand alone problem, like cancer—not on the table?

~

WHY isn't the media talking about the obvious: But for Zimmerman pursuing this lad, he wouldn't be dead! ALSO, where is the Wrongful Death suit against ALEC? But for "Stand Your Ground", pivotal in the trial, and written by this latter-day KKK, should, in kind, be sued out of existence! See: OUR GREED AND IGNROANCE, on Amazon/Kindle

~

WHY on earth would ANYONE vote Republican? The "R" for their extremists, stands for "Racists"—and the Republicans in Congress are like a child having a temper tantrum—throwing America, and the American people under the bus--to undermine President Obama See: IT IS IMPOSSIBLE TO BE A CHRISTIAN, AND VOTE REPUBLICAN, on Amazon/Kindle

~

Why on Earth would ANYONE vote Republican, today? A reptile has more decency than the Republicans in Congress! Only an odious toad would pass Ryan's budget or gut Food Stamps—and these depraved snakes made them THEIR HIGHEST PRIORITY! If only one child in America goes hungry because of the Republican's War on Children it explains why---IT IS IMPOSSIBLE TO BE A CHRISTIAN, AND VOTE REPUBLICAN, Amazon/Kindle

~

Wolf Blitzer-CNN—Those who liked Hitler and McCarthy, will love Ted Cruz—what a nothing human being! He is a consummate Republican, today, and like Paul Ryan and that ilk—

embraces an America unfit for human habitation! These are NOT DECENT people—so why don't we cut to the chase and call these radical extremists what they are? See: OUR GREED AND IGNORANCE, on Amazon/Kindle

~

Always Running in the background--and the hidden agenda at FOX [not the news], Lindberg cheezehead [you know the ones]--but at all times their agenda is to divide America into the "good guys" and the "bad guys"--and they have our ignorant thinking they are the "good guys"--so here is our slogan for this election...Vote For The Good Guys: VOTE DEMOCRAT

~

For 99.99% of those voting Republican, today, this could be compared to going to a football game and cheering for the opposing team to win....the Republicans are NOT on your side—they don't have your back—and the extremist radicals who have taken over the Republican party want to stab you in the back! Get Smart! Use your head! Vote for the GOOD GUYS:

VOTE DEMOCRAT! See: OUR GREED AND IGNORANCE, Amazon

~~~~~

CHAPTER TWO

FAIL-SAFE ELECTRONIC VOTING

TO THE READER. Given you have gotten this far, and agree with the proposed changes—and particularly given the pernicious Citizens United—our democracy, and the above, or any, progress, will be in peril absent a "fail-safe" electronic voting system. The following is my proposed solution, and like every solution proposed, here, feed-back--your proposed improvement, etc. is welcomed.

THE FAIL-SAFE ELECTRONIC VOTING ACT

1) EVERY electronic voting machine (hereafter EVM), must be inexpensive, identical throughout the U.S. in a 1/150 ratio, and *must count and produce a hard-copy of the recorded votes.* In addition, an extra copy of their recorded votes would be produced (not necessarily a hard-copy), marked "Voter's

Copy", and containing "NOTICE: Do Not Destroy Until Every Election On Your Ballot Is Certified". [If Wal-Mart handed us a piece of paper with the words "trust us" as a receipt for our purchases—we would be outraged—and yet, this is our current electronic voting nightmare—but in this case it is our democracy at risk]!

2) *After confirming that their votes are recorded correctly*, the voter would then insert the hard-copy ballot into a software-free (count only) optical scanner (hereafter OS), for a second count. The hard-copy ballot would be retained by election officials in the event a candidate asks for a recount (*not possible under the current system, and which undermines the legality of each such election*). The EVM and the OS must be manufactured by different companies (which is universally true today).

3) Election officials assigned to oversee the EVM, would be prevented by law from overseeing the OS, and vice-versa, and stiff criminal penalties would be imposed for violations.

4) Further, every EVM would be programmed with raw data re the total registration rolls, by party, and norms for their voting history, etc.,---

-as an "alert" to a possible irregularity, such as an "under-vote"—or "vote-flipping" etc., and *standards* established to suspend certification where there is an "improbable result", at least temporarily, of a particular election until the discrepancy is cleared up. (This is what computers do best, and it would be very easy to create such a program).

5) At the end of the election day, tallies would be taken from the EVM and the OS, for each candidate. *If the tallies didn't balance for any given election, or if there is an "alert", that election cannot be certified until the "error" is corrected.* If the candidates agree (the victory is certain), minor discrepancies in the count could be disregarded. While probably rare, the Voter, or a random sample of Voters, would be required by law to return their Copy of the recorded votes to the election office to clear up any "error", or where an "alert" signals the need for same.

6) Further, every state provides for a recount when the total vote falls below a certain percent of difference between the candidates, impossible to conduct with the current EVM. And thus Congress must mandate the following regarding presidential candidates: A RUN-OFF election is

mandated and triggered in those states where the percent of total vote is less than .5% of difference between the two candidates; said election to be held on the second Saturday following the election, on PAPER BALLOTS ONLY, and contain ONLY the names of the relevant candidates, for instance: "Barack Obama, Democrat" and "John McCain, Republican"—with oversight in counting by a representative(s) of each party—said procedure providing more than adequate time to meet the Electoral College mandate [Ideally, all of this could be eliminated if we did away with the Electoral College, but until then….]. NOTE: Had this been the law in 2000, Al Gore would be our president, and America would have been spared the economic, etc., disaster that followed!

7) Finally, absent the above safeguards, and until these safeguards are in place--Congress must mandate that PAPER BALLOTS, ONLY, can be used in our presidential elections. This is not a "partisan" issue, it is a "pro-democracy" issue. Most importantly, this will return the responsibility for our elections, and our vote counting, back into the hands of the individual voter, where it belongs, and out of the hands of "corporate control"---*it is* after all "our democracy", itself, that is at risk if we don't take

these steps---and in that regard, is there any time or cost differential that is too great?

Jim Green

CHAPTER THREE

I didn't write the following. It is a cut and paste from FACEBOOK, or some blog [would like to give credit if knew the author]--but it is so on target regarding how "fear" is driving Conservative policy in America today—i.e., is undermining America and our progress—and relegating America to a Third World country status, rather than a world leader—FDR had it on the nose in "All we have to fear, is fear itself"…at his inaugural in 1933….

"Conservatives are such cowards: they are afraid of gay people getting married or serving in the military; they are afraid of bringing terrorists to super max prisons in the US from which no one has ever escaped; they are afraid of the boy scouts letting gay kids in; they are afraid of everyone voting and are constantly suppressing the vote under some bogus voter fraud theory; they are afraid of letting students vote at their universities; they are afraid of women having the right to choose; they even are afraid of women getting contraception [the real issue actually is a women's agency and control over their bodies]; they are afraid of immigration reform leading to citizenship because they are afraid of-- name whatever reason; they are afraid of mandating gun purchasers to undergo background checks for crazy people and terrorists; they are afraid of people smoking pot; they are afraid of climate change being real and contradicting their beloved Bible; they are afraid of legitimate campaign reform; they are afraid of Muslims; they are afraid of blacks; they are afraid of atheists; they are afraid of hippies; they are afraid of socialists; they are probably still afraid of monsters under their beds; they are just rank cowards and keep making things up to be afraid of."

CHAPTER FOUR

[I couldn't resist including this…and yes I am the author…..]

A MESSAGE FROM GOD

MANY CENTURIES AGO, a man of the cloth, we don't know his name, and in a flash of insight (perhaps induced by peyote) told his flock that "sex is a sin". And lo and behold he learned that by taking a very natural and healthy part of our life and turning it into something that was "dirty and nasty", that he could imprison his flock, and fill his coffers, and hallelujah it was a great day for the Lord!

Quickly, his miracle spread to other churches in his village, and then to the next village, and then the next county, and then state, and soon it spread to all the churches in the ancient world, and all of their flocks cowed in fear and shame and became imprisoned, and their coffers over-floweth. Hallelujah, it was a great day for the Lord!

And to keep the myth alive they started inventing stories, half-baked stories, that made no sense to anyone who is rational, such as "Mary was a virgin"—well, she just had to be a virgin because she would never partake in anything that was dirty and nasty, like sex (if you're doing it right), and this was necessary to make "sex is a sin" make sense...so they invented a Mary that was "sinless"--you get the picture. And their coffers over-floweth. Hallelujah, it was a great day for the Lord!

No one seemed to be bothered that when we play tricks on the human mind by taking something that is very natural and healthy, such as sex, and make it dirty and nasty that all kinds of bad things happen to the human mind:

Such as most pedophiles, and most serial killers, and voting Republican, and unwarranted suicides, and most mental illness, and unwanted pregnancies. (Teens not wanting to have sex is the perversion, not the other way around, and by replacing sex education and condoms, with unrealistic "abstinence", and by using blather about "low self-esteem" to shame them into not "sinning"—We have a teen pregnancy in the U.S. twice that of England and Canada!).

But none of this mattered, because their coffers over-floweth, and Hallelujah, it is a great day for the Lord!

There is a cure--------Tell these right-wing loonies to shove it....

GOD

ABOUT THE AUTHOR: I was employed in our Criminal Justice System for a cumulative 20 years as a probation officer, with 5 of those years as a chief probation officer. I authored the concept of "Shock Incarceration" which became law in Kansas in 1970, and then was adopted in numerous jurisdictions in the U.S. and also spread to Europe—it is currently identified in the U.S. as "Boot Camp" [as the means to "shock" the young offender—and a total distortion of my original intent—like many ideas, once released, they take on a life of their own]. I also instigated establishment of the first Court Psychiatric Clinic in the U.S., in conjunction with psychiatrists from the Menninger Foundation, as a chief probation officer. Finally, I was the Democrat candidate for Congress, District 21, TX, 2000. I would most define myself as a Social Ecologist-- [albeit my degree is in Psychology]. My web page is www.Inclusivism.org –which has been on the internet since 1996.

A BRIEF ADDENDUM: When the U.S. Supreme Court denied certiorari—where the violation of my constitutional rights were obvious, and criminal negligence on the part of the government defendants in the death of our son, equally obvious—[detailed in THE HARVARD BOYS CLUB, Amazon/Kindle]--I filed a Petition for Rehearing [which is automatic]—and included the following. The Clerk of the U.S. Supreme Court called me at my work in California, and asked that I withdraw the "cartoon" [a reprint from The NEW YORKER] from my Petition. I refused on the basis of the First Amendment, and it remains in the archives at the U.S. Supreme Court [Docket #: 79-1627], to this day. The wording [not that clear] is: "Excellent, excellent. A fine blend of truths, half-truths, and blatant falsehoods".

IN THE

Supreme Court of the United States

October Term, 1979

No. 79-1627

JAMES L. GREEN,

Petitioner,

vs.

OTHER BOOKS BY THIS AUTHOR ON
AMAZON/KINDLE/BN:

- THE HARVARD BOYS CLUB: Hitler's Assault On Our Freedoms From His Grave
- MY LETTERS TO PRESIDENT OBAMA: Confessions Of A Compulsive Letter Writer
- OUR GREED AND IGNORANCE: Poses A Far Greater Threat To America, Than Terrorism
- LETTERS ON STEROIDS: Confessions Of A Compulsive Letter-To-The-Editor Writer
- THE FIRST TIME I HAD SEX: And, The Religious Intolerance Attack On America
- WHY PRESIDENT OBAMA LOST THE 2012 ELECTION: A Wake-Up Call
- ECONOMIC INCLUSIVISM: Neo-Capitalism/An Anthology: Inclusive pro-market solutions to our social problems

- AMERICA IS ONE SICK MF: Why Greed-Driven America Went Off The Rails....
- EVERY GIVEN SUNDAY: A Scientific Formula To Predict NFL Games
- And others....

www.ingramcontent.com/pod-product-compliance
Lightning Source LLC
Chambersburg PA
CBHW020538290526
45786CB00002B/932